Suncatcher

poems by

Brian C. Miller

Finishing Line Press
Georgetown, Kentucky

Suncatcher

ACKNOWLEDGMENTS

I would like to thank the following magazines and journals for their
publication for individual poems:

Nebo—"Remodeling My Heart," "When Silence Creates Questions"
Old Red Kimono—"Parachute"
Down in the Dirt—"A Magician's Glass," "The Moment," and "Fastball"
Shemom—"Road Trip," "Driving in a Small Town"
Straylight—"1988"
Floyd County Moonshine—"Traffic Jam"

Special thanks: To my mom for her unconditional love and support, to
my poetry professors at Penn State Altoona who helped hone my craft,
Ann Bickel for the author photo, and Dawn Bawa for capturing my poetry
through art.

Publisher: Leah Huete de Maines
Editor: Christen Kincaid
Cover Art: Dawn Bawa
Author Photo: Ann Bickel
Cover Design: Elizabeth Maines McCleavy

Order online: www.finishinglinepress.com
also available on amazon.com

Author inquiries and mail orders:
Finishing Line Press
PO Box 1626
Georgetown, Kentucky 40324
USA

Contents

*For all my friends who have supported me on my writing journey
for the last 20 years.*

Suncatcher

Time and age speed up
when a life event pops up,
such as my first love.
This prompted me to think
about time's speed trap:
There is not enough daylight
to make up for "loving her"
just like I dreamed.
But God gave me that time.
He fit her in my arms
like holding a suncatcher.
She reciprocates my feelings
as her porch light shines on us.
Years may go faster in my world,
but the blink of her brown eyes
are moving. Slow.

The Tattoo Artist

She's like a tattoo
painted deep within my skin.
She opened the door
to my heart. I let her inside.
She loved me for me,
and painted on my chest.
Every single memory—
Friday night dates,
hayrides and carnivals,
even my secrets
that I kept locked away.
She became a professional,
carving an outline of each letter:
H. A. R. M. O. N. Y.
The sting turned to beauty,
and blended us together.
She's always there
even when she's not
anymore.

The Experiment

Time is like the speed of light when finding a rare love.
So I tried this little experiment...

The cracking of neon flames
interrupt our conversation
during a fire pit date.
It's just me and her
as a cricket chirps
in the moon's background.
Another year is almost gone,
which reminds me: time blinks.

We hold hands and see
constellations circle the skies.
The ashes light up her green eyes,
that acts as a mirror. Stillness
matches her natural beauty.
Our stares tell a story—
I see her past heartbreaks.
She sees my past heartbreaks.

When the smoke fades,
we talk about how God
brought us together
in this fast-paced world.
But this moment of holding her,
getting to know her,
makes up for lost love.

Remodeling My Heart

When I first met her,
my trust was still broken
from the last love—
cracks all over my heart.
Little by little,
she glued the cracks
and unscrewed my guard
that I put up every day.
Her words turned to bolts,
securing me in my life.
She drilled trust in me,
and I watched hurt blow
like sawdust in the wind.

Run

We spent the summer talking
by our park bench. Topics
ran through my mind, like
Tell me about your family,
What's your favorite song?,
How I ran nowhere to find love,
and *Why do you like crafts?*
Loved how she ran her fingers
through her long brown hair,
only to roll it up again.
She talked about everything,
including her failed marriage.
The comfort levels ran on high
every time I saw her.
God answered my own prayer
when she said, *I pray every night.*
When we walked through the park,
she took a concerned, deep breath
and told me she has to move. Away.
It doesn't matter where or why…
I tried to memorize her green eyes,
and the warmth of her palm in mine.
But the days kept running away
until I ran out of time.

Magician's Glass

Trust is a fragile glass
that reflects golden light.
I poured my feelings to her
until I heard an empty silence.
I waited. Silence. I waited.
Trust is a fragile glass
that needs filled to the rim.
I only tasted a sip. The glass
starts to crack like a spider web
as pieces and parts of crystal
shatter on a concrete floor.

Road Trip

This moment depicts
my gray stubble—
A trait that reminds me
that time still blinks.

This moment also depicts
her strands of gray hair—
A reminder that we bonded
as years painted subtle face lines.

These lines acted as a road map
that came full circle. We reflect.
We open up about life's journey.
Other girls kept their feelings folded.

March

She's a spring breeze
blowing clovers on a rooftop.
I'm walking on air
backed by a pot of gold.
She's also a classic—
reminiscing of life's snapshots
like a Cadillac at a drive-in movie,
third graders playing hopscotch,
or opening a cracker jack prize
at a Cubs game.

Bioluminescence

There are magical moments that resonate from a summer love
that somehow lost its glow. I hope she remembers
this special time...

Her hand's warmth created an eye glow
when we walked around the pond.
Each step we took on blacktop
carved an iridescent path.

We discussed our busy lives
while her head rested on my chest.
When the street lights glimmered,
my eyes caught her stare with a smile.

I caught a lighting bug,
and felt like a boy
collecting those fireflies
in my backyard.

Now, I observed the black eyes
and watched the bug's glow shine
like a star on my arm.
Each crawl slowed down time

with an intimate, first-time feeling.
I felt her breath a couple of times.
She tried, but it clung to my arm
as the words, "I think he likes you"
echoed in the still summer air.

Cotton Candy Clouds

Stay home. Shutdowns. Masks.
       Pandemic 2020. Uncertainty.
To stop from overthinking,
I researched how to write a love song
thanks to a YouTube tutorial.
Didn't have anyone in mind
since becoming single again.
So I wrote "Beautiful,"
comparing her to cotton candy clouds
and the sunshine all around.
The simple little melody
made me forget about uncertainty.
If only I could find the right girl…

I kept that song in my memory files
while talking to a new girl—
Online dating and normalcy had returned.
But she was faithful. She was honest.
She met me at that pizza place
while discussing our life stories.
I told her "I love you," which was a first.
To my surprise, she said "I love you too,"
which was another first.

She came to my house for a cookout,
so I grabbed my guitar and sang "Beautiful."
She smiled to the first strum,
and her foot taped to the dreamy chorus.
Her hand shook when she held the lyrics
as cotton candy clouds moved around sunshine.

Dream

Dreaming can be memories,
like water painting
on my grandparents driveway,
or buying baseball cards after school.

Dreaming can be make believe
like becoming a millionaire,
or winning a Nobel Peace Prize.

Dreaming can be real,
like how she giggled
when I kissed her first—
A feeling I never experienced.

Dreaming can feel it's not real,
like how she had to move away,
which left me broken.

Dreaming can prompt what ifs,
like seeing her in a wedding dress.
If I had known her then,
I would have made
all her dreams come true.

Traffic Jam

Images of her memory jam
into my mind like traffic.

Her hand cream mixed
with a hint of lip gloss.

Her white tank top that hid
underneath her jean jacket.

Her soft, dreamy voice
discussing love poems.

Her handwritten heart.
Her midnight waltz.

Her makeup that washed
away from raindrops.

When Silence Creates Questions

Melancholy air touches my skin
as I open my eyes from a dream
that provided a sense of color.
But color fades to ellipses,
and silence follows me
to every corner of the house.
Endless hours on the clock blink.
It's as if doorknobs are untouched
and windows project an invisible view.
Question marks appear on the tiles
as I try to fill in the blanks.

That's Funny

Not in a haha way.
But in an interesting way
that's sealed with a smile,
and maybe a little giggle.
I dusted off this old love poem
I wrote 14 years ago.
It was about the depth
of getting to know you.
Just a poem to express
my feelings I locked inside.
Maybe the poetic words
could fill my lack of love.
As the years strung together,
you always found a way
to stick to me like glitter.
But the timing was always off-
You were too busy and beautiful.
I was scared to ask you.
Then you had a boyfriend,
and I had a brief girlfriend.
But it ended in hurt.
It's funny how you rescued me
and we ended up together anyway.

Parachute

Her memory is a parachute in high altitude,
trying to slow down time,
so I don't forget my first love.
A warning label stamps the blue sky
and reads: "Time speeds up when love is new."

Her body leaned against my shoulder
as we curled on her couch.
She thanked me for buying her a jean jacket
that covered a coat rack in the kitchen corner.
Those light blue sleeves
reminded me of her embrace,
and a safe landing.
Her bare foot brushed my arm
as a kiwi scent mixed in with air from a fan.

Discussing Libra and Sagittarius
rescued me in that moment
when she said, "That's a good match for us."
I traced around her ankle vine tattoo—
an accidental tickle made her smile.
When she discussed her daughter's dancing,
her chestnut eyes lit up.
Sunlight shined through the window
as dust particles fell on her coffee table
with a gentle landing.

Music of Faith

Sing unto the Lord a new Song
Psalm 96:1

I am stuck in the same song
like stale lyrics written on rocks.
Fear finds the chorus-a dark refrain
that echoes in minor chords.
I'm lost in convoluted noise.

But Jesus is a clever songwriter.
His songs are fresh like Sprinkling Rites
that touch down on my skin.
I raise my hands and sway.
This is my new song. My new prayer.

Driving In a Small Town

They started out as a romantic team,
attraction, at eighteen. Her blond hair rested
on his shoulder for a slow dance at the prom.
It's about time they get to know each other,
but a couple of short years later,
she's a statistic on a billboard:
"Killed by a drunk driver."

The Bronze Statue

Glorious thoughts emerge from my mind
every time I pass this statue on fourth street.

He stands five feet against stained glass.
But to me, he looks over the Earth.

His bronze hands reach out to the sky
as if to touch the world.

A tower clock stands by a Cathedral
to remind me of the value of time,

and how He has guided me every year
since I was a boy, just learning about Him.

When worries of the day wear me down,
this statue of Jesus is my lighthouse.

The Shuffle

Sometimes I feel like the Ace of Spades
shuffling through a deck of cards.

Sometimes I feel like a dice
shuffling through a gambler's hands.

Sometimes I feel like the Mona Lisa
shuffling through art galleries.

Sometimes I feel like raindrops
shuffling through a rooftop.

Sometimes I feel like a jellyfish
shuffling through a tidal wave.

Sometimes I feel like an ant
shuffling through spider webs.

Sometimes I feel like leaves
shuffling through branches.

Sometimes I feel like ice
shuffling through a fountain drink.

Sometimes I feel like a stack of quarters
shuffling through a vending machine.

Sometimes I feel like sawdust
shuffling through a drill.

Sometimes I feel like clothes
shuffling through a laundry mat.

Sometimes I feel like a stranger
shuffling through a new town.

But I always feel complete
shuffling through God's plan.

Black and White

The smell of ink on paper
resonate through this notebook.
It's like a video in my mind
as each page writes itself.
This book will be my story-
a snapshot that adds weight,
the highlight reel of my life.

Free the Melody

Sometimes you have to look into your past to find the music that shaped you...

The radio played the soundtrack
of my youth. The summer of '93:
I crushed waves in my pool
to create a hype for high school.
I wanted to fit in/make friends.

Our deck will be our new dining room
as my dad and his friends rebuilt it
through hammer and nails.
The sound of power tools faded
to the sound of a Garth Brooks song

on our basement stereo. I felt
at ease and said "enjoy being a teen"
as every song erased pounding nails.
I had a free ticket to hear these songs
that reshaped our home. My youth.

Writing Outside the Box

He gets inspiration
from a jukebox
and a jack in a box.
It's the music and winding
movement that writes itself,
the unpredictable pop
of a retro tune.

Faraway Scarecrow

I feel like the scarecrow walking
down this empty yellow brick road.
Crows follow me and chew
around my shoes because my brain
vanished under a giant rainbow.
This rainbow inhales dust
and exhales smoke in the sky.
As I try to find my path,
kids laugh and bully me,
leaving a dab of hay
on the shoulder of the road.
When the hay blows away,
pressure fills up in my head.
The sun's honey-like glow
flashes a string of memories,
like the click of a magic wand.
I see myself as a boy thinking,
running on the playground
as a hint of blacktop heats the air.

Luminous Silence

The speed of my life spins fast
as I see lines in my reflection.
So I drive to a nearby Church
and pray. Reflect. Rejoice.
Kneeling on this pew,
I glance at the cross.
Jesus creates a silent stretch
to slow down the clock.
All of my years fill the silence,
like slow motion memories
that tell me time is precious.
So Jesus finds the boy within me
as a stained-glass glow
lights up silence on my pew.
Life was young and new
like the freedom of swinging
in my backyard. Orange glows
lit up small shadow clouds
along the blue-gray sunset,
where growing old seems so far away.

The Moment

Time on our tongues
speak volumes
through air we breathe.
Earth is a blurry dot—
lost in a blanket of stars
of an unknown universe,
a long line of time.
But we wash our faces
with cool tap water
and live.

Condiments

Rejection slips slip into my mailbox.
"Thank you for your submissions,
but your poems don't add spice
for our taste at this time. Good luck."
Maybe this is why my paper
is as white as a mayonnaise jar.
Topics I write about may be cliché,
but words are red with movement
like ketchup squirting on French fries.
I find ideas from depths of sun rays
and balance the mysteries of life
like a line of mustard on a hot dog.
A paper clip holds these rejection slips—
A barbeque stain on my creativity.
But I still relish in my writing.

Fastball

The ball rolled on gravel
outside my pap's house.
I needed extra practice,
so I asked my dad
to pitch a few to me.
I imitated the stances
of several Mets players.
A steady swing worked
because it sailed back
into the dry creek.

The boy inside of me
can still remember
my dad's soft toss,
the plastic bat
swiping the wind,
and the smell of pinecones
in the circular grass.
The smallest memory
is sewn together
like the seam of a baseball.

Relief

Hurt hides behind my eyes,
and opens the door to my mind.
Holding onto grudges every day
is like a revolving door
that blocks my entrance.
But I let go of these grudges,
and let God catch me
in His safety net.

Map of Minds

Dad dropped me off at the Gap parking lot
because I never had a car in college.
I grabbed my brown backpack,
and walked to the student center
and took out a book and highlighter.
I walked around the pond
during study and class breaks.
I shook hands with my friends
while drinking coffee in the lounge.
I learned how to speak Spanish
and wrote poems about love and life
until I graduated from Penn State.
These memories resonate in my mind
just like the trees reflecting on the pond.

As the years strung together,
my dad's memory started to fade.
He can't drive or work anymore.
He forgets his birthday,
and sometimes forgets who I am.
But I will always remember dad
drinking Diet Pepsi in the morning,
coming home from the TV station,
playing the piano after dinner,
watching a movie in the basement,
and helping me get into college.
I can still hear the sound of dad's car door
where it seems like yesterday—
Dad picked me up at the Gap parking lot.

1988

If I had a View Master reel, I would see myself
as an 11 year-old boy learning about life...

My coach scratches his blond mullet,
and explains how to hit. My elbow is up.
Sweat pours down my helmet.
Bat is steady. Footprints carved in dirt.
I imagine a game-winning home run.

Click.

I relax on our brand new deck
and study the blue sky.
I wonder, "How will 5th grade go?"
as I adjust my Mets cap, thinking.
A robin visits me on the deck's pillar.

Click.

I keep long division homework
in my trapper keeper. Papers everywhere.
I look at the wooden floor. "Where's my pencil?"
My secret girl crush stares at me.
Her blue eyes match the keeper's design.

Click.

It's Christmas morning. I thumb through
a wrestling magazine. Hulk Hogan poses
on this issue. Wrapping paper dominates carpet.
My dad fiddles around with a remote. He wants
to show me how to work a VCR. I miss him.

Click.

Brian C. Miller received a BS degree in Elementary Education from Penn State Altoona in 2002. He worked for a year as a Special Education Aide and decided to return to Penn State Altoona. This time, he received a BA in English. It was here where he learned the craft of poetry. After graduating in 2005, he returned as a Special Education Aide for the Altoona Area School District

He has won several poetry contests sponsored by the Blair County Arts Foundation. In 2021, he wrote a memoir, *Patience of Faith: My Journey to Overcome Social and Academic Struggles*. It is self-published through Amazon.

This is his third chapbook published by Finishing Line Press. *The Blue and White Tent* was published in 2012 while *The Cosmic Tour* was published in 2018. His poems has recently appeared in *Nebo, Old Red Kimono,* and *Straylight*.

He enjoys music, baseball, and spending time with his friends. He is a Special Education Aide for the Altoona Area School District. He resides in Altoona, PA and can be reached on Facebook and brianmiller34@netscape.com